A Kid's Guide to

Hawaii

Curious Kids Press • Palm Springs, CA
www.curiouskidspress.com

Hawaii At-a-Glance

Official Name: State of Hawaii

Capital City: Honolulu

Total Land Area (Size): About 6,423 sq. mi. (16,635 km^2)

Population: 1,427,538 (2017)

Official Languages: English and Hawaiian

Nickname: Aloha State

Publisher: *Curious Kids Press, Palm Springs, CA 92264.*
Designed by: Michael Owens
Editor: *Sterling Moss*
Copy Editor: *Janice Ross*

Table of Contents

Chapter 1

ALOHA!
Welcome to Hawaii

ALOHA. Are you ready to hit the beaches in Hawaii? There's probably no better place on Earth for scuba diving, snorkeling, and surfing!

But Hawaii is much more than just fun in the sun. Before you jump in the water, take a quick tour of this fascinating U.S. state – the 50th state of the Union.

WHERE IN THE WORLD IS HAWAII?

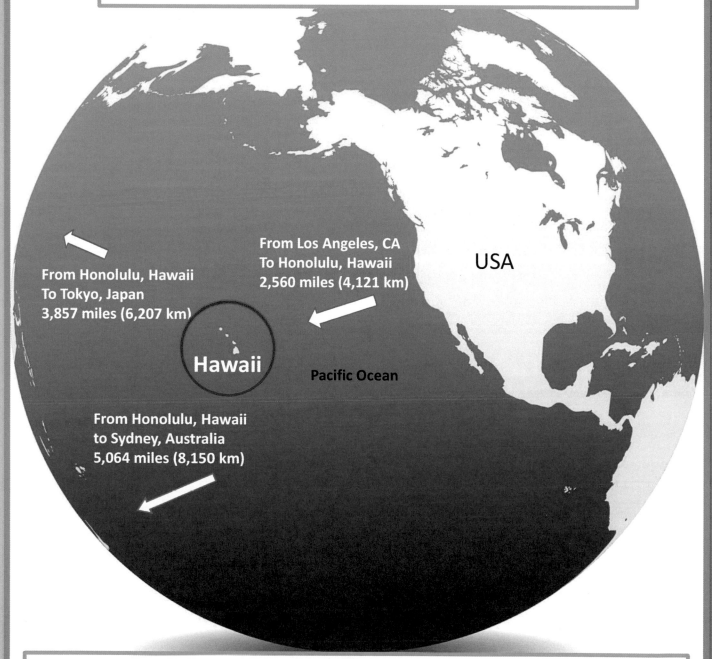

From Honolulu, Hawaii
To Tokyo, Japan
3,857 miles (6,207 km)

From Los Angeles, CA
To Honolulu, Hawaii
2,560 miles (4,121 km)

USA

Hawaii

Pacific Ocean

From Honolulu, Hawaii
to Sydney, Australia
5,064 miles (8,150 km)

HAWAII IS LOCATED in the Pacific Ocean, 2,560 miles (4,121 km) from Los Angeles, California. It is an **archipelago** made up of 132 islands, **atolls**, and reefs. It stretches more than 1,500 miles (2,414 km) from the Big Island of Hawaii to the Kure Atoll in the northwest.

Hawaii consists of eight main islands, but people live on only seven of them. You can read more about the islands of Hawaii starting on page 11.

A Brief History of Hawaii

450-600 AD: Polynesian voyagers from Tahiti arrive by canoe in Hawaii. They begin the Hawaiian civilization.

1778: British explorer Captain James Cook arrives at Waimea Harbor, Kauai. He names the islands the Sandwich Isles in honor of the Earl of Sandwich. Cook is the first European to explore the Hawaiian Islands.

1810: Chief Kamehameha (1782 – 1819) takes over all of the islands and becomes the first ruler of the Kingdom of Hawaii.

1820: Christian missionaries arrive in Hawaii and teach English. They also help create an alphabet for the Hawaiian language.

1835: The first sugar plantation is built.

1866: A deadly disease called leprosy (now called Hansen's Disease) spreads through the Hawaiian population. Those with the disease are sent to the island of Molokai to live totally separated from everyone else.

1893: The U.S. forces Queen Liliuokalani to abdicate (give up) her position of power. It does away with Hawaiian Parliament, and installs a group of American businessmen as the leaders of the new government.

1898: Hawaii becomes a territory of the United States.

1935: Amelia Earhart becomes the first person to fly solo from Hawaii to the mainland of the United States.

December 7, 1941: The Japanese attack Pearl Harbor on the island of Oahu, Hawaii. The U.S. enters World War II.

1946: A 54-foot (16.4 m) high tsunami sweeps over the east side of the Big Island of Hawaii, causing a national tragedy.

1959: Hawaii becomes the 50th U.S. state.

Cool Facts About Hawaii

Hawaii is the only U.S. state made up entirely of islands.

In Honolulu (the capital of Hawaii), it is against the law to text (or read a text) while crossing the street.

The 'Iolani Palace in Honolulu is one of only two royal palaces on U.S. soil. The other is on the Big island of Hawaii.

Hawaii is the southernmost state in the United States.

Hawaii is the only state in the Union to celebrate a holiday honoring a monarch. King Kamehameha Day is celebrated on June 11th.

Did You Know?
Hawaii was once its own country known as the Kingdom of Hawaii.

In Hawaii, there is a hand gesture that has many meanings. The gesture is called a SHAKA.

If someone does something good or cool, you can give them a shaka as a sign of approval.

It can also be used to say hello or goodbye or even thank you.

To make a shaka:
1 Make a fist (not a tight fist).
2. Stick out both your pinky (your little finger) and your thumb.
3. Lightly shake your hand.

President Barack Obama, who was born in Hawaii, gives the crowd a shaka.

Admissions Day
(aka "Statehood Day") is an important holiday in Hawaii. It celebrates Hawaii's becoming the 50th state of America in 1959. It is celebrated on the third Friday of August each year.

Some Hawaiian words are made up entirely of vowels, and all Hawaiian words end in a vowel.

Did You Know?
It is quite common to take your shoes off before entering a home in Hawaii.

Urban Legend
You may have heard there are no snakes in Hawaii. Not true. What is true is that snakes are not native to Hawaii. They have been brought to the island from other places. The most common snake is the Island Blind Snake from the Philippines. But look close. You can easily mistake it for a worm.

When trying to get around in Hawaii, there are two words you have to know for directions anywhere:

Mauka (*mow-kah*): On the mountain side

Makai (*mah-kigh*): On the ocean side

They're used by locals all the time to point you in the right direction.

Hawaii is the only U.S. state that has two official languages: English and Hawaiian.

Hawaii has the shortest alphabet in the world – only five vowels and eight consonants. (Read more about the Hawaiian language on page 30.)

The Big Island of Hawaii is bigger than all seven of the other Hawaiian islands put together.

Island	Area (sq. mi. /km²)	Islands	Area (sq. mi. /km²)
Hawaii	4,028/10,432	Maui	727/1,882
		Oahu	597/1,546
		Kauai	552/1,429
		Molokai	260/673
		Lanai	141/365
		Niihau	70/181
		Kahoolawe	45/116.5
TOTAL	4,028 sq. mi. 10,432 km²	TOTAL	2,392 sq. mi. 6,195 km²

Hawaii is one of only four states that have laws against billboards. (Alaska, Maine, and Vermont are the other three.)

Chapter 2

The Islands of Hawaii

HAWAII CONSISTS OF EIGHT MAIN ISLANDS, although people live on only seven of them.

The island of **Kahoolawe** is the smallest of the eight islands and is uninhabited. No one lives there full time.

Niihau is the smallest of the **inhabited** islands. It is about the size of Washington, D.C., or only slightly bigger than Bermuda. Only about 100 people live there.

On the next pages, you can read about the other islands, including **Hawaii** (aka the Big Island), **Maui**, **Oahu**, **Kauai**, **Molokai**, and **Lanai**.

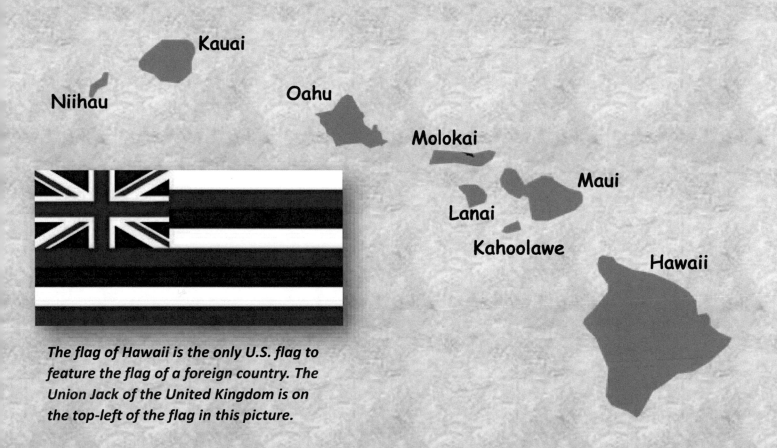

The flag of Hawaii is the only U.S. flag to feature the flag of a foreign country. The Union Jack of the United Kingdom is on the top-left of the flag in this picture.

Hawaii

The Big Island

THE NAME OF THE STATE IS HAWAII. But Hawaii's biggest island is also called Hawaii. So it can become a little confusing. That's why most people call the island of Hawaii the Big Island. It just makes everything easier to understand.

So, how big is the Big Island? Well, it is almost twice as large in size as the rest of the main islands put together. (*See chart on page 10*.) It is about half the size of the state of New Jersey or about the same size as the island of Jamaica.

**The Big Island
At-a-Glance**
(Largest Hawaiian Island)
Land Area: 4,028 sq. mi. (10,430 km²)
Populations: 185,079
Largest City: Hilo (*say: he-low*)
Fun Fact: The Kilauea Volcano is on the Big Island and is one of the most active volcanoes in the world.

On the Big Island, Akaka Falls is a stunning 442 feet (135 m) tall waterfall.

6

Maui

The Valley Isle

**Maui
At-a-Glance**
(2nd largest Hawaiian Island)
Land Area: 727 sq. mi. (1,883 km^2) About half the size of Rhode Island, USA
Population: 154,834
Largest City: Kahului
Fun Fact: Haleakala is Maui's most famous volcano and is the largest **dormant** volcano in the world. The crater at the summit is 21 miles across.

MAUI GOT ITS NICKNAME – the Valley Isle – because it sits between two mountains. The island has more than 80 beaches, including white sand, black sand, and red sand beaches. But what's there to do after surfing and swimming all day? Plenty.

Try whale-watching in Maui between January and early April. (*See page 36*). Or visit Maui's Surfing Goat Dairy on the beautiful slopes of Maui's Haleakala volcano. Or enjoy a train ride on an old open-air Sugar Cane Train that used to carry sugar from the field to the harbor back in the sugar plantation days. Or for a really thrilling adventure, go for an underwater submarine tour to see the amazing sea life of Hawaii up-close.

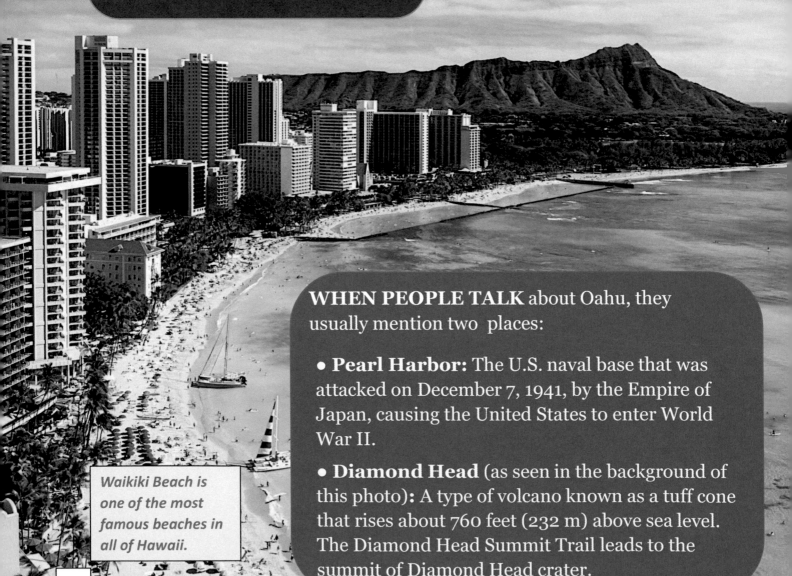

Oahu

The Gathering Place

**Oahu
At-a-Glance**
(3rd Largest Hawaiian Island)
Land Area: 596 sq. mi. (1,545 km²)
Population: 976,372
Largest City: Honolulu (also the state capital)
Fun Fact: Oahu has the only royal palace in the United States.

Waikiki Beach is one of the most famous beaches in all of Hawaii.

WHEN PEOPLE TALK about Oahu, they usually mention two places:

● **Pearl Harbor:** The U.S. naval base that was attacked on December 7, 1941, by the Empire of Japan, causing the United States to enter World War II.

● **Diamond Head** (as seen in the background of this photo): A type of volcano known as a tuff cone that rises about 760 feet (232 m) above sea level. The Diamond Head Summit Trail leads to the summit of Diamond Head crater.

Kauai

The Garden Isle

The Open Ceiling Cave is also known as Pukalani, a Hawaiian word for "hole into the heavens." It is one of the biggest tourist attractions in Kauai.

Kauai At-a-Glance
(4th Largest Hawaiian Island)
Land Area: 562 sq. mi. 91,456 km²)
Population: 68,689
Largest City: Kapaa
Fun Fact: No building on Kauai can be taller than a coconut tree.

HOP IN YOUR OWN KAYAK and paddle the warm waters of the Wailua river – Kauai's largest and longest river. Then, hike through a lush rain forest, and swim at a secluded (or hidden) waterfall.

You can do all that on the island of Kauai – the fourth largest of Hawaii's main islands.

Photo Credit: Hawaii Tourist Authority (HTA)/Tor Johnson

Lanai

The Private Isle

**Lanai
At-a-Glance
(6th Largest Hawaiian Island)**
Land Area: 140.5 sq. mi. (364 km²)
Population: About 3,000
Fun Fact: Was once known as the Pineapple Island because it produced more than 75% of the world's pineapples.

IMAGINE A PLACE where there is not a single traffic light in the whole town – or, in this case, on the whole island.

That place is Lanai, the sixth largest of the eight Hawaiian islands and the smallest inhabited island in the state of Hawaii.

In 1922, a man named James Dole purchased Lanai. Soon, the little island was producing 75 percent of all the pineapple in the world. In October 1992, the final harvest of pineapple took place on Lanai.

Today, there's plenty to do in Lanai – from watching turtles and Spinner dolphins at Hulopoe Beach to swimming with dolphins, to visiting Shipwreck Beach where you'll find this old Navy fuel barge (*see above*).

Molokai

The Friendly Isle

**Molokai
At-a-Glance
(5th Largest Hawaiian Island)**
Land Area: 260sq. mi. (670 km^2
Population: 7,345
Fun Fact: Molokai has some of the highest cliffs in the world.

Molokai Light, the lighthouse on Molokai, was built in 1909 and is 138 feet (42 m) tall.

THE FRIENDLY ISLAND OF MOLOKAI is known for many things – the world's highest sea cliffs (measuring up to 3,900 feet), Hawaii's longest waterfall, and one of the largest white sand beaches in the state.

But for many years, from the 1860s to 1969, it was also known as the home for people who had a serious disease called Hansen's disease (then known as leprosy).

Today, only about 7,000 people live on Molokai. But more than 60,000 tourists visit each year.

Chapter 3
Things for Keiki (Kids) to Do in Hawaii

1 **VISIT THE UNDERWATER WORLD of** Hawaii's most beautiful sea life at Maui Ocean Center. You'll see manta rays, sharks, and hundreds of other Hawaiian fish at this large tropical **aquarium**.

Credit: Hawaii Tourism Authority (HTA)/ Tor Johnson.

2 **SNORKEL** with green sea turtles (*honu*) on Oahu's North Shore.

3 **LEARN TO KITEBOARD on Maui** on Kite Beach, probably the best known kiteboarding beach in the world.

4 **Ride horseback** to a hidden valley waterfall at Silver Falls Ranch on Kauai.

5 GO FOR A THRILLING zipline tour on the slopes of Haleakala volcano on Piiholo Ranch on Maui..

6 **VISIT THE ONLY RAIN-FOREST ZOO** in the United States on the Big Island of Hawaii. At the **Panaewa Rainforest Zoo and Garden** in Hilo, you will see a lot of rare birds, monkeys, sloths, and lemurs, as well as a rare white Bengal tiger.

7

CHECK OUT HALONA BLOWHOLE on Kauai, where a scene from *Jurassic World: Fallen Kingdom* was filmed.

8

DIVE 100 FEET (30 m) below the surface of the sea in a submarine tour off the coast of Maui. Experience not only amazing underwater sea life, but a replica of a century-old whaling ship.

Photo Credit: Hawaii Tourism Authority/Deeja Fallas

9

MARVEL AT THE BREATH-TAKING SIGHT of Kauai's Waimea Canyon, often called the Grand Canyon of the Pacific.

10 **EXPLORE THE SUMMIT** of Kilauea volcano, one of the most active volcanoes in the world on the Big Island of Hawaii.

Photo Credit: Island of Hawaii Visitors Bureau (IHVB)/Paul Zizka

Halemaumau Crater, Kilauea Caldera, Hawaii Volcanoes National Park

KILAUEA (an Hawaiian word meaning "much spreading") is an active volcano on the Big Island of Hawaii. It is one of the most active volcanoes in the world. It has been in a constant state of **eruption** since 1983.

Lava from the volcano dribbles down into the sea. There, it hardens, causing the island of Hawaii to expand. Between 1983 and 2002, the island of Hawaii grew by 543 acres (220 ha).

MAUNA LOA, another major volcano on the island of Hawaii, is said to be the largest volcano on Earth. The last time Mauna Loa erupted was from March 24 to April 15, 1984.

Chapter 4

The People and the Customs

Statue of Kamehameha I (aka Kamehameha the Great), the founder and first ruler of the Kingdom of Hawaii .

CAPTAIN JAMES COOK (1728 - 1779)

IN JANUARY 1778, a British explorer named James Cook made landfall at Waimea harbor in present-day Kauai. Cook name Kauai and the surrounding islands the "Sandwich Islands." The islands were named for Cook's friend, the Earl of Sandwich, a British statesman. And, yes, it is the same Earl of Sandwich who is given credit for inventing the sandwich.

When Cook first arrived on the Hawaiian Islands in 1778, there was an estimated population of between 250,000 and 800,000 people. But one hundred years later,

the number of residents had dropped – drastically – to fewer than 40,000. What happened?

As other Europeans traveled to the new islands, they brought with them many diseases, such as smallpox and measles. Much of the native Hawaiian population died from these diseases.

Today, only about 140,000 people identify themselves as being "Native Hawaiian" alone.

CAPTAIN JAMES COOK (1728 – 1779)

How Hawaii Got Its Name

For 40 years, the Hawaiian Islands were known as the Sandwich Islands. But in 1819, King Kamehameha I, united the islands under his rule. He named his new kingdom "the Kingdom of Hawaii." Many people believe the name Hawaii comes from the Hawaiian word *Owhyhee*, meaning homeland.

QUEEN LILIUOKALANI (1838 – 1917)

QUEEN LILIUOKALANI WAS HAWAII'S FIRST QUEEN. She was also the last ruler of the Hawaiian islands before the U.S. **annexed** the islands in 1898.

She was born in Honolulu in 1838, the daughter of a high-ranking advisor to King Kamehameha III.

In 1874, when Queen Liliuokalani was 36 years old, her brother was named king. Liliuokalani soon became **heir apparent**.

During the next few years, she worked to improve the lives of the Hawaiian people, including starting schools for Hawaiian children.

In January 1891, Liliuokalani's brother died and she became Queen.

After the U.S. annexed the country, Queen Liliuokalani was put under house arrest. For the next several months, she was not allowed to leave her home.

Finally, in 1895, the Queen agreed to abdicate (or give up) her throne in exchange or her freedom. She died on November 11, 1917, at the age of 79.

As a young girl, Queen Liliuokalani was known as Lydia.

DUKE KAHANAMOKU (1890 – 1968)

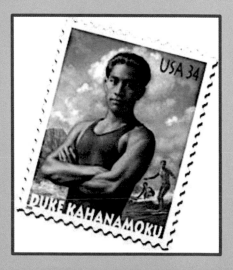

Duke Kahanamoku wasn't a "real" duke – at least, not in the sense of a *royal* duke. His first name was actually Duke and he was the first person to introduce surfing to the world.

As a young boy, Duke learned to surf using a surf board that was 16 feet (4.9 m) long and weighed 144 lbs. (52 kg).

But Duke Kahanamoku wasn't just an amazing surfer. Between 1912 and 1932, Duke competed in four Olympic Games and won six medals, three of them gold.

In 2002, the U.S. Post Office honored this amazing Hawaiian with a first-class postage stamp.

The HaWaiiaN HuLa DaNce

YOU'VE PROBABLY HEARD OF THE HULA DANCE. (You may have even tried dancing the hula.) It is one of Hawaii's oldest traditions. It tells a story with hand movements and footwork and the swaying of hips. Every year, there are major hula contests on almost every Hawaiian island.

The traditional hula costumes included a lei (a flowered necklace), a pau (skirt), and an anklet bracelet made of whalebones or dogteeth. The anklet bracelets were considered to be a musical instrument

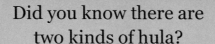

Did you know there are two kinds of hula?

The Hula Kahiko is the traditional hula. In the old days, the hula was danced on a platform, which had an altar to the goddess Pele on it.

The Hula 'auana is the name of a modern hula. It tells a story or describes a place through the movement of arms, feet, and hips.

The Hawaiian Lei

WHEN POLYNESIANS FIRST ARRIVED in Hawaii, they brought with them many important traditions.

One tradition was the lei. (*Say: lay.*) A lei is a wreath or garland made of flowers, leaves, shells, or nuts. It is worn around the neck or on the head.

In the early 1900s, tourists began coming to Hawaii by ship. Lei **vendors** met the visitors (*malihini*) at the pier and presented them with a lei to welcome them to the islands.

When the visitors left, they would throw their lei into the sea in hopes that, like the lei, they too would return to the islands some day.

Today, people give a lei at special occasions, such as birthdays, anniversaries, weddings and graduations. The lei is a true symbol of Hawaii, and an important part of Hawaiian history and tradition.

3 Rules for Giving and Wearing Leis

1. When giving a lei, remember to kiss the cheek of the person you are giving it to.

2. Never remove your lei in front of the person who gave it to you. That is considered rude.

3. Wear the lei draped over your shoulders, letting it hang down both in front and back.

And remember: Never throw a lei into the trash. That is like throwing away the love of the person who gave you the lei.

Instead, hang it on a tree branch or bury it.

The Hawaiian Luau

THERE IS PROBABLY NOTHING more truly "Hawaiian" than a luau. (*Say: LOO-ow.*)

In old Hawaii, a luau was a great celebration that would often last for days to honor ancestral gods with song, dance, and food.

Today, a luau celebrates accomplishments, honors important people, and **commemorates** great events, like high school graduations or weddings.

It is a fun time to enjoy family and friends with traditional Hawaiian food and authentic Hawaiian music, not to mention some fabulous dancers doing (what else?) the hula or fire dance.

How the Luau Came to Be

Years ago, men and women in Hawaii were not allowed to eat together. They ate their meals separately. Also, women were not allowed to eat certain foods.

But in 1819, King Kamehameha II thought the law should be changed. So he held a feast where he ate alongside women. This feast was the beginning of the present-day luau.

At sunset, every evening throughout the beachfront neighborhoods of Honolulu, a special tradition takes place. It's called torch-lighting. A young man runs down the street with a stick of fire in his hand. His job is to light the torches. He announces the torch lighting by blowing a trumpet-like Hawaiian conch shell.

Photo Credit Island of Hawaii Visitors Bureau/Kirk Lee Aeder

The Hawaiian Language

Kumu: Teacher

ohana (oh-ha-na): Family

Mahalo (ma-ha-low): Thank you.

Aloha (ah-low-ha): Hello, goodbye, and lots of other things

'Ae (sounds like "eye"): Yes

Hoaloha: Friend

'aina (EYE-nah): Food

Hau'oli lā Hānau: Happy Birthday

Kanaka he'e nalu: surfer

Keiki: Kids

Photo Credit Hawaii Tourist Authority (HTA)/Daeja Faris

THE HAWAIIAN LANGUAGE is one of the oldest languages in the world still spoken today. But one hundred years ago, it almost became **extinct**. Almost no one in Hawaii spoke it any more. Why?

In 1898, Hawaii became a territory of the United States. The Hawaiian language was banned in schools and in government. As a result, the number of people who could speak the language dropped.

But then in 1978, the Hawaiian government made Hawaiian an official language of the state, along with English. Suddenly, many Hawaiians wanted to learn the language.

Today, many schools teach some classes partly in Hawaiian. Look above at some common Hawaiian words and phrases.

Why Is There an Apostrophe in Some Hawaiian Words?

Have you ever seen what looks like an apostrophe in the word *Hawai'i*? It's not really an apostrophe, though it does look like one. It's called an *'okina*. It's found between two vowels in Hawaiian words, as in *Hawai'i*, or at the beginning of some words. It means there is a slight pause in the sound when a word is spoken. Sort of like saying "uh-oh." For example, a Hawaiian word for a type of lava is **a'a**. You pronounce it "ah-ah." The 'okina is not always used in print, so we've not used it in this book.

Fun Fact: The Hawaiian language does not distinguish between singular and plural in writing. So, for example, the word lei is both singular and plural.

Did You Know?

The Hawaiian alphabet has only 13 letters: five vowels and eight consonants. A, E, I, O, U, H, K, L, M, N, P, W, 'okina.

Did You Know?

The word Wikipedia comes from the Hawaiian word "wiki." (*Say: wee-key.*) It means fast or quick. Some schools in Hawaii have a "wiki lunch" in their schedules – which is something between a snack and a lunch during the first recess.

Try **Saying** This:

Humuhumunukunukuapua'a

(It's the name of Hawaii's state fish.)

Say: who-moo-who-moo-new-coo-new-coo-ah-poo-ah-ah

See! It's easy!

Games, Food, Holidays and More!

Games in Hawaii

Play 'Ulu maika

Want to play a game that Hawaiians played hundreds of years ago? Try 'ulu maika. It's like bowling, only with a lava rock or hockey pock or even bocce ball.
Here's how to play:

How to Play:

1. Place two stakes in the ground 6 inches (15 cm) apart.

2. Stand about 15 feet (4.5 m) back from the stakes.

3. Roll your rock, pock, or ball between the stakes.

4. Whoever rolls their rock, stone, or bocce ball the farthest wins.

Optional: Make the game more difficult by placing pairs of sakes along a path. A player must roll his or her ball between all pairs of stakes.

Holidays in Hawaii

The Merrie Monarch Festival is an annual festival that celebrates Hawaiian culture, including the hula, chanting, lei-making, and the history of Hawaii.

The first festival was held in 1886 to celebrate King David Kalakaua's 50th birthday with a two-week celebration. It was called the Merrie Monarch's Jubilee.

Today, the highlight of the Merrie Monarch Festival is a three-day hula competition.

Food in Hawaii

Hawaiians Love Spam
(.food, not unwanted emails)

In fact, the people of Hawaii eat more Spam than any other group of people in the world – other than Guam. Spam is served a lot of different ways – at breakfast with fried eggs, for lunch with mayonnaise, or for dinner stir-fried with cabbage.

Ride the Waves

Do you ever dream of riding the waves? There is probably no better place to do that than Hawaii.

Surfing was born in Hawaii – hundreds of years ago. Native Hawaiians rode wood planks and called it wave sliding.

At that time, there were certain beaches just for royalty or ali'i (*say; Ah-LEE-ee*) to surf. The regular people (or commoners) would surf at different beaches. They were not allowed to drop into the same wave as royalty.

One member of royalty who was well known for his surfing ability was King Kamehameha I. He is one reason why surfing got the nickname the "sport of kings."

Today, surfing is a favorite sport in Hawaii. Almost every island offers surfing lessons, where you can learn the basics of the sport and ride the waves.

Grab a Bite – Loco Moco

Sure, there's McDonald's in Hawaii when you're ready for fast food.

But if you want a truly Hawaiian fast food, try Loco Moco -- (*say: loh-koo-moh-koo*) – a popular fast food that can be found throughout Hawaii.

In 1949 a group of teenagers in Hawaii decided they wanted something different from a typical sandwich. They wanted something that was inexpensive and could be fixed quickly.

Two restaurant owners in Hilo, Hawaii came up with an idea. They put rice in a bowl, a hamburger patty over the rice, and added some brown gravy. To top it off they added an egg – on top. The teenagers loved it. They named the dish Loco Moco – "loco," which is Spanish for crazy (their idea was pretty crazy, right?), and Moco because -- well, because it rhymed with loco.

Today, loco moco is popular throughout Hawaii.

BTW, "moco" means "booger" in Spanish.

Chapter 5
The Wildlife of Hawaii

PLEASE
DO NOT
FEED

Nēnē
Crossing

HAWAII IS HOME to some amazing wildlife. Many of the animals are found only in Hawaii. They are **endemic** to the state. On the next three pages, you can read about some famous animals of Hawaii.

Nēnē (aka Hawaiian Goose)

It's Hawaii's state bird and the world's rarest goose. There are only about 1,000 left in the wild, so it is against the law to hunt this bird.

The nene (*say: nay-nay*) is about 16 inches (41 cm) tall . Males can weigh up to 7 lbs. (about 3 kg).

You'll find wild populations of this bird on the Big Island, as well as Oahu, Maui, and Kauai.

Photo Credit: Island of Hawaii Visitors Bureau/Kirk Le Aeder

The Hawaiian Honeycreeper

The Hawaiian Honeycreepers are found only in the forests of the Hawaiian Islands. When first born, they have a golden color. But soon, they turn bright red with black wings and a black tail.

Did You Know?
Hawaii has more **endangered species** than any other state in the United States.

THE HUMPBACK WHALE

The humpback whale is not endemic to Hawaii. In fact, these marine mammals live in oceans all around the world.

In the summer, many humpback whales lives along the Pacific Coast. But, as winter approaches, they make a 3,500 mile (5,632 km) journey to the warm waters of Hawaii. There, they will spend from November to May to breed and give birth to their young.

Did You Know?
Male whales make loud musical sounds, known as whale songs. Scientists aren't sure what these sounds mean or why only males make them. What do you think?

When a humpback whale is born, it weighs about 3,000 pounds (1,360 kg) and ranges from 10 to 16 feet (3 to 4.8 m) long. Adults can grow to between 40 and 52 feet (12 and 15.8 m) in length and weigh up to 90,000 pounds (40,823 kg).

BTW, an adult African elephant only weighs about 12,000 pounds (5,433 kg).

HAWAIIAN MONK SEALS

'Ilio-holo-i-ka-uaua (ee-lee-o holo ee ka ooa-ooa) meaning 'the dog that runs in rough waters'

Found only in Hawaii, the Hawaiian Monk Seal is critically endangered. There are only about 1,100 in the waters of Hawaii. The greatest number can be found on Kauai. But if you see one, stay a safe distance away. They can bite when disturbed.

HAWAIIAN MONGOOSE

By the late 1800s, Hawaii had become a huge producer of sugarcane. But there was one big problem. Rodents. The rodents would eat the sugarcane. Plantation owners needed something to control the growing rodent population.

So, in 1872, sugarcane farmers brought some mongooses to the Big Island. The farmers hoped the mongooses would control the rodents. (Quick Note: Yes, the plural of mongoose is mongooses, not mongeese. Odd, huh?)

As it turned out, the mongooses weren't very good t controlling rodent. Why? Mongooses are *diurnal*. They are awake during the day. Rats are *nocturnal*. They sleep during the day and are active at night.

Today, the mongoose can be found on all major islands except Lanai and Kauai.

A mongoose is one of only four mammals that has immunity to snake venom.

GREEN SEA TURTLE

The Green Sea Turtle, called *honu* in Hawaii, is the most common sea turtle in the waters of Hawaii. These large, gentle marine reptiles are typically 2-3 feet in shell length and weigh about 350 lbs (158.7 kg).

Sea turtles don't like crowds of people. So, they might be hard to spot on the beach. But there are national parks on Kauai and the Big Island that provide opportunities to see these magnificent creatures. But remember: When in the water or on the beach, please stay at least 10 feet (3 m) away from all sea turtles. It's for your safety and the animal's protection.

3 Fun Facts About Sea Turtles

1. Sea turtles are air breathing **reptiles**. That means they need to come up to the surface every so often to breathe.

2. When a turtle is resting, it can hold its breath for two hours or more.

3. Sea turtles can swim at speeds of 25 mph or more.

Glossary

Archipelago (*noun*): A large body of water containing many islands.

Annex (*verb*): To add territory to an existing nation. *The United States annexed Texas.*

Aquarium (*noun*): A place or container where aquatic forms of life are kept for exhibit.

Atoll (*noun*): A ring-shaped island or reef that surrounds a lagoon (a shallow saltwater area by the sea).

Commemorate (verb): To honor the memory of something with a special celebration.

Endemic (*noun*): Something endemic is original to or found only in a certain place.

Eruption (*noun*): The act of exploding out of a confined area. *Lava erupts from a volcano.*

Extinct (*noun*): No longer existing.

Heir apparent (*noun*): One who has a legal right to inherit a title or property.

Inhabit (*verb*): To live in or on; use as a home.

Mammal (*noun*): Any animals with a backbone that feed their babies with milk from their mothers.

Monarch (*noun*): A ruler, such as a king or queen.

Reptile (noun): Cold-blooded animal, such as a turtle, snake, lizard, or crocodile, that breathes with lungs and has short legs or none at all.

Vendor (*noun*): A person who sells things.

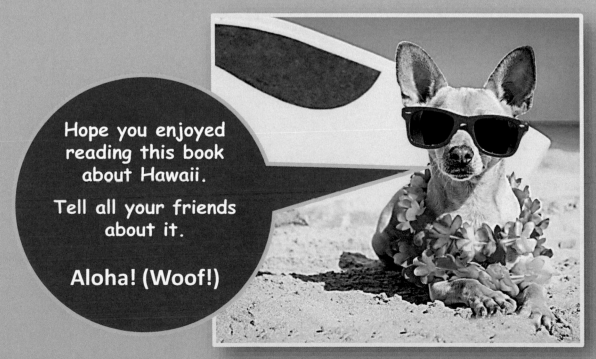

Hope you enjoyed reading this book about Hawaii.

Tell all your friends about it.

Aloha! (Woof!)

Explore the World

Find these books on Amazon.com
Preview them at curiouskidspress.com

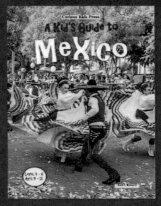

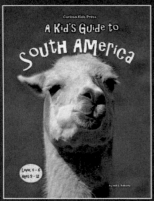

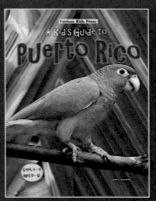

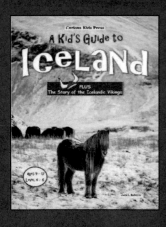

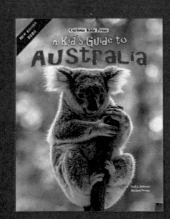

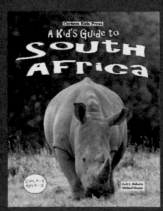

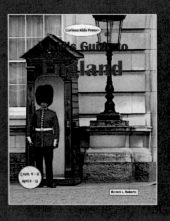

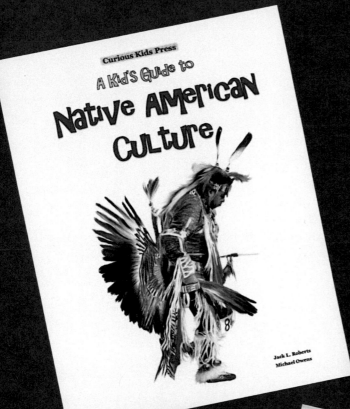
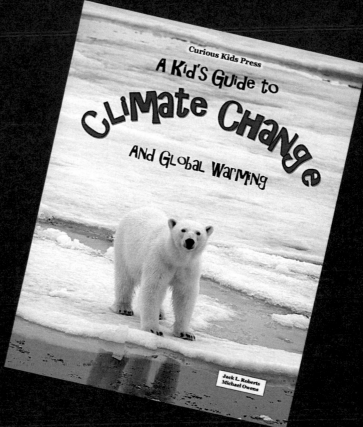

A Kid's Guide to
HAWAII
For Parents and Teachers

About This Book

A Kid's Guide to . . . is an engaging, easy-to-read book series that provides an exciting adventure into fascinating countries and cultures around the world for young readers. Each book focuses on one country, continent, or U.S. territory or state, and includes colorful photographs, informational charts and graphs, and quirky and bizarre "Did You Know" facts, all designed to bring the country and its people to life. Designed primarily for recreational, high-interest reading, the informational text series is also a great resource for students to use to research geography topics or writing assignments.

About the Reading Level

A Kid's Guide to . . . is an informational text series designed for kids in grades 4 to 6, ages 9 to 12. For some young readers, the series will provide new reading challenges based on the vocabulary and sentence structure. For other readers, the series will review and reinforce reading skills already achieved. While for still other readers, the book will match their current skill level, regardless of age or grade level.

About the Authors

Jack L. Roberts began his career in educational publishing at Children's Television Workshop (now Sesame Workshop), where he was Senior Editor of The Sesame Street/Electric Company Reading Kits. Later, at Scholastic Inc., he was the founding editor of a high-interest/low-reading level magazine for middle school students. He also founded two technology magazines for teachers and administrators.

Roberts is the author of more than two dozen biographies and other nonfiction titles for young readers, published by Scholastic Inc., the Lerner Publishing Group, Teacher Created Materials, Benchmark Education, and others.. More recently, he was the co-founder of WordTeasers, an educational series of card decks designed to help kids of all ages improve their vocabulary through "conversation, not memorization."

Michael Owens is a noted jazz dance teacher, award-winning wildlife photographer, graphic arts designer, and devoted animal lover.

In 2017, Roberts and Owens launched Curious Kids Press (CKP), an educational publishing company focused on publishing high-interest, nonfiction books for young readers, primarily books about countries and cultures around the world. Currently, CKP has published two series of country books: "A Kid's Guide to..." (for ages 9-12 and "Let's Visit . . ." (for ages 6-8) — both designed to help young readers explore the wonderful world of diversity in everything from food and holidays to geography and traditions.